HISTORIC KILSYTH

HISTORIC SCOTLAND

HISTORIC KILSYTH

Archaeology and development

E Patricia Dennison, Gordon Ewart, Dennis Gallagher
and Laura Stewart

THE SCOTTISH BURGH SURVEY

CBA
COUNCIL FOR BRITISH
ARCHAEOLOGY

North
Lanarkshire
Council

THE UNIVERSITY OF EDINBURGH

Edited by Martin Brann, Historic Scotland

Page design and typesetting by Carnegie Publishing Ltd.

Printing and Binding: The Alden Press, Oxford

Historic Scotland acknowledges with gratitude the contribution from North Lanarkshire Council towards the publication of this volume.

ISBN: 1-902771-57-5

EAN: 978-1-902771-57-1

Council for British Archaeology

St Mary's House

66 Bootham

York

YO30 7BZ

www.britarch.ac.uk

Historic Scotland

Longmore House

Salisbury Place

Edinburgh

EH9 1SH

Tel. 0131 668 8600

Fax. 0131 668 8669

www.historic-scotland.gov.uk

Front cover images: Aerial view of Kilsyth town centre, looking south, 1991

(By courtesy of RCAHMS; © Crown copyright RCAHMS)

Market Square, early twentieth century

(Reproduced by permission of North Lanarkshire Council Museums and Heritage Service;

© North Lanarkshire Council Museums and Heritage Service)

Contents

Figures

Abbreviations

APS	*Acts of the Parliaments of Scotland* T Thomson and C Innes (eds) (Edinburgh, 1814–75)
BL	British Library
DES	*Discovery and Excavation in Scotland*
NAS	National Archives of Scotland
NLS	National Library of Scotland
NMRS	National Monuments Record of Scotland
NSA	*The New Statistical Account of Scotland* (Edinburgh, 1845)
OSA	*The Statistical Account of Scotland 1791–99* Sir John Sinclair (ed) New edition I R Grant and D J Withrington (eds) (Wakefield, 1978)
Proc Soc Antiq Scot	*Proceedings of the Society of Antiquaries of Scotland*
RCAHMS	Royal Commission on the Ancient and Historical Monuments of Scotland
RMS	*The Register of the Great Seal of Scotland* J M Thomson *et al* (eds) (Edinburgh, 1882–1914)
SRS	Scottish Record Society
Third Stat Acc	*The Third Statistical Account of Scotland, 18: Ayrshire* R C Rennie (ed) (Glasgow, 1966)

Acknowledgements

We are grateful to individuals with local knowledge of Kilsyth who have given their time to assist with this survey; our thanks go to Morag Cross, Jim Bolton from the Kilsyth History Society, Agnes Valentine along with the staff at Kilsyth Library, and also to Carol Swanson. We would like to thank Pat Kelly from North Lanarkshire Council for his assistance and the Planning & Environment Department for providing details of the forthcoming work on the pedestrianisation of Main Street.

Particular thanks go to John Gordon of Kilsyth Academy. Mr Gordon's unrivalled local knowledge was invaluable to the survey and his efforts on our behalf are greatly appreciated.

The staff at Historic Scotland, the Royal Commission on the Ancient and Historical Monuments of Scotland, the National Monuments Record of Scotland, the National Library of Scotland Map Library, and the National Archives of Scotland have all assisted in the production of this work.

The survey would not have been possible without the research carried out by Dr Winifred Coutts and Dr Margaret Munro. Figures 1, 3, 15, 22, and 25 were produced by Kirkdale Archaeology Ltd and the broadsheet was designed by Headland Archaeology Ltd.

Research for this survey was conducted in the winter of 2003/04 by the Centre for Scottish Urban History at the University of Edinburgh and Kirkdale Archaeology. The Survey of Historic Kilsyth was entirely funded by Historic Scotland. Historic Scotland acknowledges the generous contribution of North Lanarkshire Council towards the cost of publication.

1   Use of the Burgh Survey

The third series of Burgh Surveys is intended both as a guide for the general reader to the rich history and archaeology of Scotland's historic burghs and to furnish local authorities with reliable information to help protect and manage the archaeology and historic environment of our urban centres. This Survey provides an accessible and broad-ranging synthesis of existing knowledge on historic Kilsyth, as well as highlighting research areas that would benefit from more detailed analysis.

In its role as a tool for local authorities to use in the planning process, the first point of reference in this volume is the colour-coded town plan (**fig 25** and **broadsheet**) which depicts the areas of prime archaeological interest. The general index will enable rapid access to information specific to a site, street or feature within the town.

Further information on the archaeological potential of a site or area within the town can be gleaned from local and national libraries and archives. The PASTMAP website (http://www. PASTMAP. org. uk) can also be consulted. This interactive website, supported jointly by Historic Scotland and the Royal Commission on the Ancient and Historical Monuments of Scotland, allows anyone with internet access to display and search data on Scotland's historic environment, and particularly the legally protected sites – scheduled ancient monuments and listed buildings.

Both this Burgh Survey and the PASTMAP website provide information only. Where development is being considered, in all cases advice should be sought from the Local Authority planning department, and from their archaeological advisers: for North Lanarkshire, the West of Scotland Archaeology Service (Charing Cross Complex, 20 India Street, Glasgow, G2 4PF; telephone: 0141 287 8333) should be contacted.

2 Site and setting

Geographical location

Kilsyth lies at a height of 60 m above sea level near the confluence of the Garrell Burn and the Ebroch Burn, tributaries of the River Kelvin, midway between Glasgow and Stirling (**fig 1**). The town centre is on north-facing land (**fig 2**); the Kilsyth Hills rise steeply to the north beyond the Garrell Burn while to the south is the valley of the River Kelvin, and beyond it the ridge of Bar Hill and Croy Hill. The Kelvin valley is very marshy, especially at Dullatur Bog to the south-east of the town, and until the building of the Forth & Clyde Canal (**fig 3**), it formed more of a barrier than a communication corridor. The town lies on the 'long road from Glasgow to Edinburgh',[1] now known as the A803. It sits on the intersection with the old hill road from Stirling, known as Tak Ma Doon Road (**fig 3**), and the route south to Cumbernauld via Auchinstarry Bridge.[2]

Kilsyth was formerly in the county of Stirlingshire. In 1975, it became part

FIGURE 1
Location map: Kilsyth and
surrounding area
*(Prepared by Kirkdale
Archaeology; based on OS
mapping © Crown copyright.
All rights reserved. Historic
Scotland licence no. 100017509
[2006])*

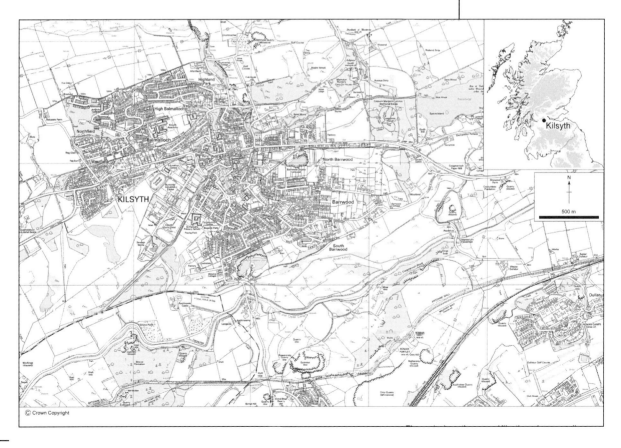

© Crown Copyright

FIGURE 2
Aerial view of Kilsyth town
centre, looking south, 1991
(By courtesy of RCAHMS;
© Crown copyright RCAHMS)

of the Cumbernauld & Kilsyth district of Strathclyde and since 1995 it has been part of the North Lanarkshire Council area.

Geology

Kilsyth is situated in the northern part of the Midland Valley of Scotland, the relatively low-lying central part of the country between the Grampian Highlands and the Southern Uplands. Central Scotland has a complex geological history with a wide variety of rocks and physical features reflecting this. The rich mineral sources of the area played a significant role in shaping the history of the town.

Kilsyth lies on the north-west edge of the wide basin of carboniferous limestone of the central coalfield, where it terminates against the volcanic mass of the Campsie Fells and the Kilsyth Hills (**fig 1**). This limestone is rich in mineral resources, especially coal. The best-known seam in the district was

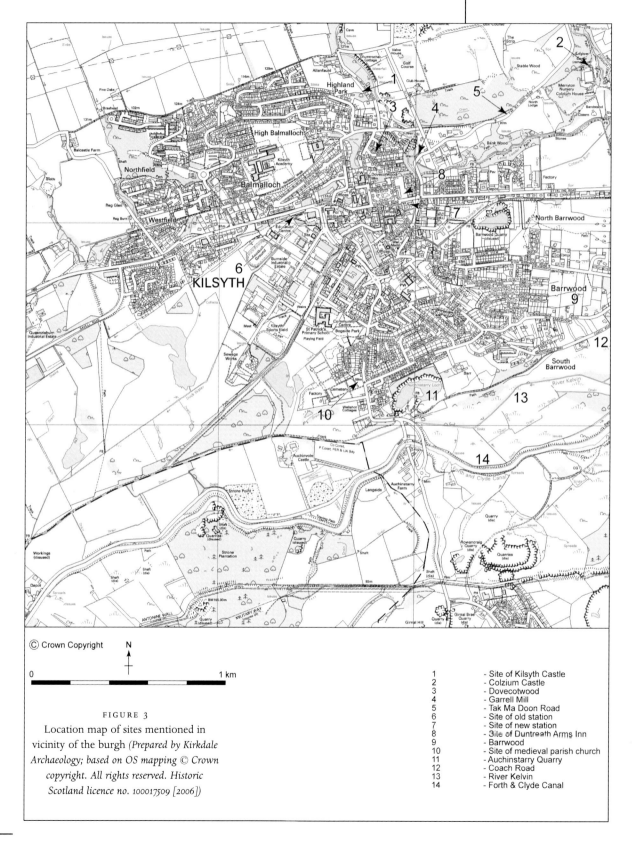

N

0   1 km

FIGURE 3

Location map of sites mentioned in
vicinity of the burgh *(Prepared by Kirkdale
Archaeology; based on OS mapping © Crown
copyright. All rights reserved. Historic
Scotland licence no. 100017509 [2006])*

1	- Site of Kilsyth Castle
2	- Colzium Castle
3	- Dovecotwood
4	- Garrell Mill
5	- Tak Ma Doon Road
6	- Site of old station
7	- Site of new station
8	- Site of Duntreath Arms Inn
9	- Barrwood
10	- Site of medieval parish church
11	- Auchinstarry Quarry
12	- Coach Road
13	- River Kelvin
14	- Forth & Clyde Canal

the Kilsyth coking coal, which was at its thickest to the north-east of Kilsyth and outcropped at Banton, *c* 3 km east of Kilsyth. The geological structure is modified by faulting and by subsidiary folding, the most conspicuous features of which are the Campsie and the Milngavie-Kilsyth faults (the latter running east–west to the north of the town). This landscape is modified by igneous intrusions; Kilsyth itself is built on an intrusive quartz-dolerite sill, the Barr, which forms a distinctive landform in the upper Kelvin valley and provides a much-quarried source of 'whinstone'.

The landforms have been shaped by extensive glaciation; in the last 120,000 years the area has seen five periods of partial covering with ice-sheets. The valley east of Kilsyth has a landform of mounds and hollows created by glacial erosion and deposition. During deglaciation, meltwater rivers formed deep channels that are a feature of the present landscape.[3]

Soils

The best agricultural land is along the broad valley of the Kelvin and neighbouring slopes, but drainage is difficult and flooding frequent. To the south and east of the town there are brown fluvioglacial sands and gravels derived from carboniferous sediment. Elsewhere is a till derived from carboniferous sandstone and a boulder clay subsoil, resulting in a soil that is very heavy for agricultural uses.[4]

Climate and land use

In 1792, the minister of Kilsyth parish, Mr Robert Rennie, described the climate as 'in a certain degree moist', but without the fogs of the east coast or the 'almost incessant rains' of the west.[5] The land of the parish ranges from the boggy land in the Kelvin valley bottom to the upland pastures of the Kilsyth Hills (**fig 1**). After 1715, the land was leased in farms that each extended

FIGURE 5
Extract from William Roy's
Military Survey of Scotland,
1747–55 (By permission of the
British Library; Sheet C9b5)

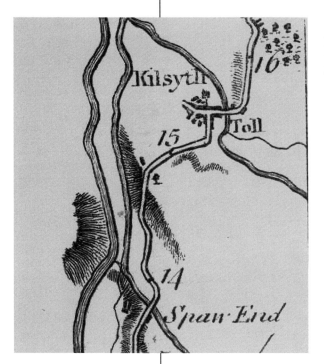

from the Kelvin valley north to the hills, with the lands of the valley bottom being unenclosed. The long north–south boundaries of these farms can be seen on the mid-eighteenth-century map by William Roy (**fig 5**).[6] The agriculture was therefore mixed arable and pastoral, although the amount of arable was said to have declined after 1715. In the eighteenth century, the rearing of Highland cattle for the market at Falkirk predominated.[7] The principal arable crop was oats, with barley, beans, potatoes, and rye grass also grown. Potatoes, originally cultivated only in gentlemen's gardens, were grown as a field crop for the first time in Scotland at Kilsyth in 1739 and rapidly gained in popularity after that date.[8] The land in the Kelvin valley was improved in the 1780s by an extensive drainage programme instigated by Sir Archibald Edmonstone of Duntreath.[9] By 1841, further land had been enclosed with hedgerows and Ayrshire cows had been introduced, their dairy produce finding a ready market in the town.[10]

Topography and physical setting of the burgh

Prior to the establishment of a burgh of barony in 1620, the settlement that became Kilsyth was situated by the banks of the Garrell Burn and its tributary, the Ebroch Burn (**fig 3**).[11] The more level land to the south of this was utilised for the regular layout of the burgh.

Sources of evidence

Sources describing the town of Kilsyth, particularly during the early stages of its development, are limited. Papers generated by the forfeiture of the Kilsyth estate after 1715 provide information about the size of the town and its inhabitants, although most of the material relates to the rural parts of the estate.[12] The entry for Kilsyth in the *Statistical Account of Scotland*,[13] originally written in 1795 and updated in the mid-nineteenth and late twentieth centuries, provides detailed material both on the parish and the town. This can be usefully supplemented by the Report of the Commissioners on Municipal Corporations, which describes Kilsyth's political structures as established by 1836.[14]

A number of nineteenth- and twentieth-century sources could be used to trace Kilsyth's industrial heritage, which has been introduced only briefly in

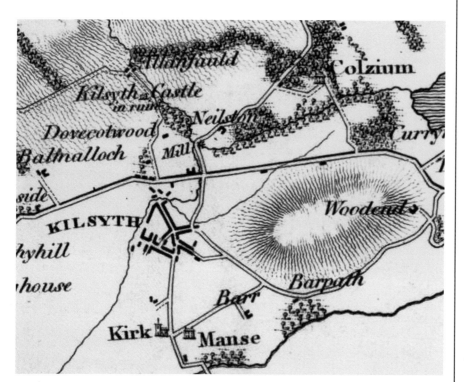

FIGURE 7
A detail of John Grassom's
map of 1817 *(Reproduced by
permission of the Trustees of the
National Library of Scotland)*

this survey. North Lanarkshire Archives in Cumbernauld hold council records for Kilsyth, which cover much of the nineteenth and twentieth centuries. The now-defunct Coal Board, Kilsyth's numerous friendly societies, the railway companies, and the Scottish Office all generated material relating to Kilsyth's industrial development.[15]

The earliest cartographic depiction of settlement in the Kilsyth area is on the manuscript map of *c* 1580 by Timothy Pont (**fig 4**).[16] Robert Gordon's manuscript map of Stirlingshire, drawn *c* 1636–52, is based on that of Pont and gives no more information.[17] The layout of the town is clearly depicted by William Roy in his *Military Survey* of 1747–55 (**fig 5**) and on the map of the Antonine Wall published in his *Military Antiquities of the Romans in Britain*.[18] A map of 1764 relating to the planning of the Forth & Clyde Canal shows some details of Kilsyth and the surrounding area.[19] A road map of 1776, by George Taylor and Andrew Skinner (**fig 6**),[20] shows the earlier road to the east of the town. Maps, by Ross in 1780,[21] John Grassom in 1817 (**fig 7**),[22] John Thomson in 1820,[23] and John Ainslie in 1821,[24] show a simplified plan of the town and its relationship with the present A803 to the north; that of Thomson appears to be a somewhat inaccurate copy of Grassom's map.

A more detailed plan of the town was published by local historian Hugo Millar in his *History of Cumbernauld and Kilsyth from the Earliest Times* (1980). Millar entitled the map 'Kilsyth 1679: The original 45 feus',[25] but the source on which it was based is unknown. Neither Colzium House nor the National

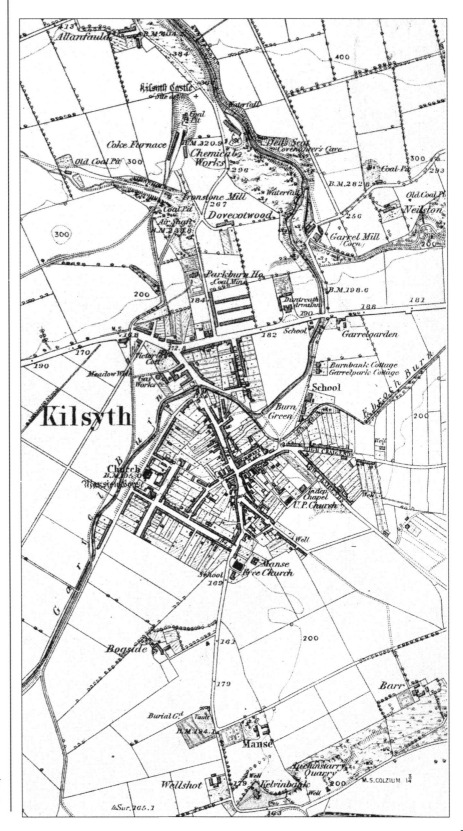

FIGURE 8
Detail from the 1st Edition of
the Ordnance Survey 1:10,560
map of 1865

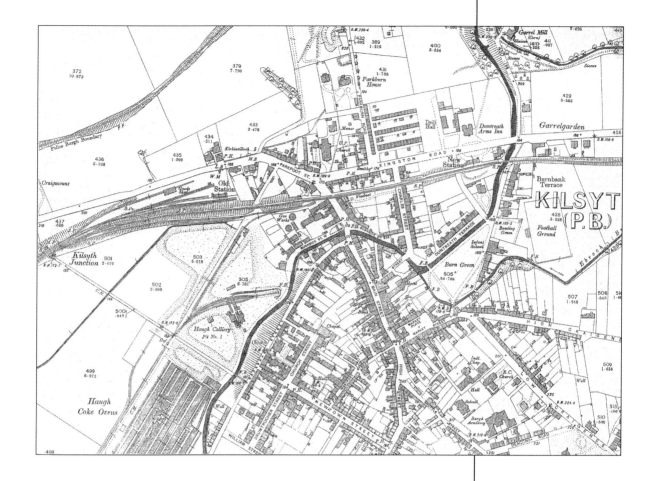

FIGURE 9
Detail from the 2nd Edition
of the Ordnance Survey
1:2500 map of 1898
(By courtesy of RCAHMS)

Archives of Scotland, which keeps papers relating to the Kilsyth estate, possess any material that might have been used to create the map. It is possible that Millar had access to an undiscovered source dating to the late eighteenth century; Meeting House Lane (later U P Road) (**fig 15**), named after the Relief Church founded there in 1768, was included,[26] but Newtown Street, dating from the early nineteenth century, was not. Whatever its origins, the map almost certainly cannot be attributed to any seventeenth-century source.

Cartographic sources from the nineteenth and early twentieth centuries are particularly useful for looking at Kilsyth's physical expansion and development. Sir Archibald Edmonstone's estate plan of 1856 shows the town in considerable detail.[27] The Ordnance Survey maps, with editions showing Kilsyth produced in 1865 (surveyed 1859) (**fig 8**) and 1898 (**fig 9**), can be used to chart the nineteenth-century expansion of the town.[28] The development of part of Shuttle Street (**figs 9 & 15**) can be traced from a series of block plans in the National Archives of Scotland, although only one is dated.[29] The architectural record of the National Monuments Record of Scotland also has photographs of a number of buildings in Kilsyth.

Notes

1. W Roy, *The Military Antiquities of the Romans in Britain* (London, 1793), no XXXV

2. RCAHMS, *Stirlingshire: An Inventory of the Ancient Monuments* (Edinburgh, 1963), 423–4

3. I B Cameron and D Stephenson, *British Regional Geology: The Midland Valley of Scotland* (London, 1985), 64, 70, 106, 119

4. T Robertson and D Haldane, *The Economic Geology of the Central Coalfield. Area 1 Kilsyth and Kirkintilloch* (Edinburgh, 1937), 3

5. *OSA*, ix, 412

6. W Roy, *Military Survey of Scotland, 1747–55*, BL, C9b5

7. *OSA*, ix, 470–2

8. *OSA*, ix, 474–8

9. *OSA*, ix, 413–17

10. *NSA*, viii, 157

11. *OSA*, ix, 438–9

12. NAS, CS129–63, Acts of Sequestration, Kilsyth Estate, 10 July 1716; NAS, E640/1, Rental of the Estate, 1716–19; *Abstract of the Rental of the Real Estate of William late Viscount of Kilsyth, in the Shire of Stirling,* (Edinburgh, 1719). The latter can be located in the NLS.

13. *OSA,* ix, 407–509; *NSA*, viii, 138–68; *Third Stat Acc*, 18, 273–90

14. R Handyside, 'Report on the Burgh and Barony of Kilsyth', *Reports of Commissioners on Municipal Corporations, Scotland* (London, 1836)

15. NAS, CB series (Coal Board), FS series (records of the friendly societies), BR series (British Rail), and DD series (Scottish Office Development Department). See also the RHP series, showing plans of the Kilsyth area relating particularly to coal deposits.

16. NLS, Adv Ms 70.2.9, T Pont, 'Map of the East Central Lowlands' (Pont 32)

17. NLS, Adv Ms70.2.10, J and R Gordon, 'Sterlinshyr & Lennox. Sterlingshyre, wt a part of the Lennox, and sum of Clydsdal' (Gordon 50)

18. Roy, *Military Survey*, C9b5; Roy, *Military Antiquities*, no XXXV

19. J Smeaton, *A plan of the tract of country between the Forth and Clyde ...*, 1764, Royal Society Archives, JS/6/64. Microfilm copy in the NMRS.

20. G Taylor and A Skinner, *A General Map of the Roads, Made Out of Actual Surveys taken out by Geo Taylor and Andrew Skinner* (London, 1776)

21. NLS, C Ross, 'A Map of Stirlingshire, 1780'

22. NLS, EMS. s. 623, J Grassom, 'To the Noblemen and Gentlemen of Stirling' (Edinburgh, 1817)

23. NLS, EMS. s. 712(14), J Thomson, 'Stirlingshire' (Edinburgh, 1820)

24. NLS, EMS. s. 712(14), J Ainslie, 'Map of the southern part of Scotland, 1821'

25. H B Millar, *History of Cumbernauld and Kilsyth from earliest times: including a guide to places of interest in the district* (Cumbernauld, 1980), 62

26. J Gordon, *Kilsyth History Trail* (Kilsyth, 1980), 7

27. NAS, RHP 46700, Plan of part of the estate of Kilsyth, adjoining the town of Kilsyth, 1856. A reduced copy can be found at NAS, RHP 46699.

28. Ordnance Survey, 'Stirlingshire', 1st edn, 1:10,560 scale (sheet XXVIII, 1865); Ordnance Survey, 'Stirlingshire', 2nd edn, 1:2500 scale (sheet XXVIII, 1898)
29. NAS, RHP 82526–32, Architectural block plans of subjects in Shuttle Street and Pirnie Street, Kilsyth

3 History and archaeology

Little archaeological work has been undertaken within the historic core of Kilsyth. An introduction to the prehistoric, Roman, and early historic development of the area has, therefore, been included to provide a broader framework within which to study the origins and development of the burgh.

Prehistory

The earliest settlement of Scotland occurred *c* 7000 BC, when much of the country was covered in dense woodland which supported a rich variety of game, particularly red deer. The few Mesolithic (literally meaning Middle Stone Age) settlements known in Scotland tend to be found along the coastline and riverbanks. These communities were 'hunter-gatherers' who ate fish and shellfish, followed herds of woodland game through the seasons, and supplemented their diet with wild plants and berries. Their semi-nomadic existence has left few archaeological traces, although shell middens and flint tools are common finds along former rivers and coastline. Finds of Mesolithic

FIGURE 10
Orange Lodge (11 High Street) and Gospel Hall (3 Market Close) prior to demolition in 1985
(By courtesy of RCAHMS;
© *Crown copyright RCAHMS)*

implements are rare in central Scotland but this may reflect a comparative lack of fieldwork rather than a genuine absence.

Around 3500 BC (the Neolithic/New Stone Age), people began to live a more settled existence, partly in response to changes in the climate. Large areas of woodland were cleared by burning and trees were cut down with stone tools. Livestock was kept and land farmed for crops. Ritual played an important role in the lives of these early farming groups, particularly in their treatment of the dead, who were buried in monumental tombs. These communal stone-built chambered cairns or barrows constructed of wood and turf sometimes contained large numbers of burials. These tombs may also have become a focus for ritual, perhaps with elaborate ceremonies being performed there to commemorate ancestors. Remains of a chambered cairn survive at Craigmaddie (NS 5859 7646), 9 km west of Kilsyth.[1] A Neolithic polished stone axe was found at Braehead Farm (NS 7049 7867), 2 km north-west of Kilsyth;[2] another polished stone axe was found near Croy (NS 730 756).[3]

FIGURE 11
Panel dated 1764 on Gospel Hall, 3 Market Close
(By courtesy of RCAHMS; © Crown copyright RCAHMS)

By c 2500 BC (late Neolithic / early Bronze Age), changes in society were gradually taking place. The tradition of monumental tombs containing large numbers of burials waned in favour of a new trend for single grave burials. A number of burial mounds that formerly existed in the vicinity of Kilsyth are likely to have been from this period. Some are known to have contained cremation urns. Mounds are recorded as having existed at Auchincloch (NS 767 789), Kelvinhead (NS 757 786), and near Chapel Green (NS 695 774).[4]

Considerable changes in technology and in society took place at the end of the Bronze Age, c 600 BC. Iron tools and, increasingly, weapons appear in the archaeological record. Despite the abundance of evidence for monuments and rich burials in the Neolithic and Bronze Age, knowledge of the subsistence base which supported these societies, and the settlements in which they lived, is rather poor. By the late Bronze Age / early Iron Age, however, settlements begin to dominate the archaeological landscape. Numerous fortified settlements, ranging from large hillforts to enclosed villages and isolated single-family dwellings, are known. Less-defensive types of settlement also existed, but the remains from this period may reflect a more competitive society, in which groups perhaps fought over natural resources. The impression is that there was a move away from large monuments that served the community in the second and third millennia BC, towards settlements indicative of tribal division. Finds from this period from the vicinity of Kilsyth include a middle Bronze Age flanged axe (NS 733 765)[5] and a late Bronze Age ribbed socketed axe, both found near Croy (NS 72 75).[6]

Later prehistoric and Roman periods

It was this fragmented society that the Romans encountered in AD 80, when Agricola, the governor of the Roman province of Britannia, sought to extend Roman control northward. They promptly established a network of fortifications and communication routes throughout southern Scotland which ensured their effective control of the native tribes. According to Ptolemy, the classical geographer writing in the second century AD, the Kilsyth area lay in the northern territory of the Damnonii tribe.[7] Evidence for native settlement of this period in the Kilsyth area is in the form of duns, or small fortified settlements. Gordon, writing in the early eighteenth century, described a small fort with a stone rampart at 'Columbee'. The structure no longer exists but the site has been identified as the hillock in the Colziumbea plantation (NS 7391 7774), 2 km east of Kilsyth.[8] Another small hillfort survives at Castle Hill (NS 7091 7610) on the south side of the River Kelvin, close to the Roman fort of Bar Hill.

The coming of the Romans had a huge impact on the Kilsyth area. Around AD 90 the overstretched Roman army had to withdraw troops from Scotland and a new defensive line was established between the Tyne and Solway,

which was consolidated in the AD 120s with the construction of Hadrian's
Wall. Renewed expansionism under the Emperor Antonius Pius (AD 138–61)
saw the abandonment of Hadrian's Wall in favour of the Antonine Wall and
its associated chain of forts along the Forth-Clyde line. This turned the Kilsyth
area into a militarised frontier zone.

The Antonine Wall was built on the south side of the Kelvin valley, 1.5 km
south of Kilsyth, the marshy valley bottom serving as an additional obstacle
in the frontier defences. The Roman forts of Bar Hill (NS 707 759) and Croy
Hill (NS 733 765) are visible from the town. Part of a Roman altar was found
in the course of excavations at Kilsyth Castle (NS 7173 7865) in the 1970s. The
worn inscription was identified as that of an altar taken to the castle c 1605,
where it was seen at that date by the antiquarian William Camden.[9] The
North Lanarkshire area's second period of Roman jurisdiction was, however,
relatively short-lived and by the AD 160s Hadrian's Wall had resumed its role
as Rome's northern frontier.

Native circular fortifications, probably duns of late Iron Age or early
historic date, were recorded near Kilsyth towards the end of the eighteenth
century, at Auchinvalley (NS 742 791) and Townhead (NS 740 782);[10] no traces
of these remain today. A larger structure, possibly a broch, was recorded in
1727 near Auchincloch (NS 76 79). This had a circular stone wall of c 4 m in
height and 5 m in thickness, enclosing an area of c 25 m in diameter.[11] The
apparent density of settlement of this period in the south-east of the parish
may relate to the lighter, more easily cultivated soils of that area.

The early historic period

From the seventh to the ninth centuries Kilsyth lay between the territories of
the Scots of Argyll, the Picts of eastern Scotland, and the Northumbrians of
Lothian. The first church was situated in a settlement known as Monyabroch,
to the south of the present town
(NS 7168 7720). No remnants of the church building survive above ground
level. The site of the church and the earlier graveyard form the north-eastern
part of the present cemetery, where burial continued after the parish church
was moved to another site in 1816. The church may be an early foundation
although, as with the former Central region of Scotland in general, there is
an absence of the early Christian sculpture that normally indicates early
church foundations.[12] Chapel Green, Queenzieburn (NS 695 774), c 2.5 km
west of Kilsyth town centre, has been suggested as the site of an early
medieval church, although there is little evidence to support this claim and
there are no visible remains.[13] There are a number of holy wells in the vicinity
of Kilsyth that may have been cult centres from the early medieval period.
One of these is St Mirren's Well (NS 7232 7956), where one source claims there
are remains of what may have been a fifth-century monastic cell.[14] The well

is now enclosed within a later building and the water piped. A nearby stone (NS 7232 7957) bears the date 1687.[15] Another well, documented in the late eighteenth century, was called St Tartan's.[16]

The medieval period

The land that was later to be Kilsyth lay in the eastern part of the earldom of Lennox. The parish was known as Monyabroch, but part of this district was known as Kelvesyth by at least the beginning of the thirteenth century. In 1216 Maldoven, earl of Lennox, granted to Malcolm, son of Duncan, the lands of Glaswel and a plough and a half in Kilsyth.[17] A new grant, including 'Monaeburgh, Kilsyth, Glaswell and Callander', dates from c 1239.[18] This was confirmed by King Alexander III (1249–86) in 1251 and included the church of 'Moniabrocd'.[19] The lands of Kilsyth appear to have passed at some point into the hands of the Callendar family, who were forfeited in the early fourteenth century for supporting the opponents of King Robert I (1306–29). A marriage between the Callendar heiress and Sir William Livingston resulted in Sir William acquiring a charter, dated 1362, for his wife's former inheritance.[20]

The founder of the Livingston family of Kilsyth was William Livingston. A younger son of Sir John of Callendar, he was married in 1421 and gained as his patrimony the lands of Wester Kilsyth. Both William and his heir, Edward, appear as 'of Balcastel' as well as 'of Kilsith'.[21] The remains of at least two residences which may date from this period are still visible in these areas today. Castlehill, Colzium (NS 7350 7823) (**fig 3**), c 1.8 km to the east-northeast of Kilsyth and the motte of Balcastle (NS 7011 7818), c 1.8 km to the west-northwest of Kilsyth, both sit on natural knolls.[22] Stone foundations also existed for a property known as 'Old Place', near Queenzieburn (NS 6904 7781), which was ruinous by the 1740s.[23]

The sixteenth century

At the beginning of the sixteenth century, the Livingstons seem to have built a new residence. Fragments of Kilsyth Castle (NS 7173 7865) (**fig 3**) survive on the north side of the burgh at Allanfauld. Archaeological excavation has shown that the castle was originally built c 1500 as an L-shaped tower. Its short west wing had been considerably enlarged in 1605, according to a dated sill stone recovered from the debris.[24] The castle is clearly depicted on the late sixteenth-century manuscript map of Stirlingshire by Timothy Pont. It shows an L-shaped tower with adjacent wing surrounded by a barmkin wall and within enclosed wooded parkland (**fig 4**).[25] The property was destroyed during the English invasion of 1650. Its remains, up to 1 m high in places, can still be seen on the west side of Allanfauld Road, south of Allanfauld Farm (NS 7173 7865). In recent years, the site has been assessed by Kilsyth Academy Field

Archaeology Group.[26] Another late sixteenth- or early seventeenth-century moated L-plan tower house was erected at Auchenvole (NS 7138 7690), south of the town in the Kelvin valley. It appears to have been built by a family called Stark, whose superiors were the lords Fleming. The property was incorporated into a Victorian mansion but this was demolished in 1977 and no visible remains survive, apart from outbuildings and a dovecot.[27]

Timothy Pont's map (**fig 4**) also shows the scatter of fermtouns that formed the pre-burghal settlement in the Kilsyth area. Burnside is shown in the confluence of the Garrell Burn and the smaller Ebroch Burn. Another unnamed settlement is marked on the south side of the Garrell Burn, in the approximate position of the present Kilsyth town centre. To the south, the kirk of 'Monyabrach' is shown, with Bar and Colzium ('Colyam') to the east of the church. Pont's map, as well as numerous later ones, also show a settlement called Nealstoun lying between Kilsyth Castle and Colzium. It seems to have disappeared before the early nineteenth century.[28]

A modern investigation has been conducted of building foundations behind the south-east corner of High Street and Market Street (NS 718 777) (**fig 15**). This uncovered the remains of a late sixteenth-century farmhouse that had been incorporated into the burgh and subsequently re-used as a dyeing establishment for weavers.[29] Its central position in the burgh, at the intersection of two roads, suggests that the agricultural settlement formed an existing nucleus, which expanded when the burgh was planned. This settlement may be identified with the unnamed place shown on the late sixteenth-century Pont map, north of Monyabroch kirk (**fig 4**).[30] The medieval parish church of Monyabroch was situated to the south of this small settlement, in what is now the town cemetery.[31] It lay under the patronage of the earls of Lennox as early as the early thirteenth century. By the Reformation of 1560, it was in the hands of Lord Livingston of Callendar.[32] During the 1560s, the incumbent could expect to take possession of 'two arable acres of land with a small house for room'.[33]

The seventeenth century

In 1620, Sir William Livingston of Kilsyth, senator of the College of Justice and privy councillor, consolidated the lands of Kilsyth and Monyabroch. At the same time, Sir William was given the right to establish a burgh of barony at Kilsyth.[34] The size of the burgh at this period is unclear. The *Statistical Account* claims that in the early years of the seventeenth century, Sir William Livingston of Kilsyth bought the land around the Garrell Burn 'for the express purpose of extending the village'. Prior to this, the village had been clustered around the Ebroch Burn.[35] Apparently the burgesses were given the right to dig peat on the slopes of Garrell Hill and to dry or bleach linen on the areas of common land at Burngreen and Backbrae.[36]

By mid-century, it seems this development was well under way (**fig 22**):

A new town was built, not along the banks of the Ebroch or Garrell Burn as formerly, but on rising ground about 200 yards south of those streams, which at that time was called Moat Hill, as the Lord of the manor had been accustomed to hold courts of justice in that place. This new town of course was called by the title of the proprietor, Kilsyth.[37]

On 16 August 1645, forces fighting for King Charles I (1625–49) under the command of James Graham, 1st Marquis of Montrose, met those of the Scottish Covenanters under Lieutenant-General William Baillie, just to the east of Kilsyth. Montrose was victorious on this occasion. Local place-names such as Bullet Knowe (NS 743 780) and Slaughter Howe (NS 737 792) act as grim memorials of that day, while it is alleged that bones belonging to the fallen continued be found on the site in the nineteenth century.[38] The site of the battle (NS 7395 7855) has disappeared under the reservoir for the Forth & Clyde Canal.[39]

Due to its strategic location between Glasgow and Edinburgh, the Kilsyth area suffered greatly during the civil wars of the 1640s. The lands of Easter

FIGURE 13
Market Chambers, 1977
(By courtesy of RCAHMS;
© Crown copyright RCAHMS)

and Wester Kilsyth were destroyed in 1645 by Montrose, despite the royalist sympathies of the incumbent, Sir James Livingston of Barncloich, future Viscount of Kilsyth and Lord Campsie. His lands 'lay waste' in 1646, and had troops quartered on them in 1648.[40] In 1650, Kilsyth was burnt by 'the Usurpers armie' headed by Oliver Cromwell, and the following year, forces fighting for King Charles II (1649–85) requisitioned Livingston's goods. While he was in prison in 1654, the mansion was burned again, by 'Hielanderis' who wanted to prevent it becoming a garrison for the English, who occupied Scotland until 1660.[41] A reminder of these turbulent times stands against the wall of the parish church on Backbrae Street (NS 7161 7779). Reputedly a gravestone, engraved with the initials FC and the date 1646, it was moved to its current location in 1892.

The Livingston residence at Kilsyth, later known as the 'old mansion' or the 'mansion house' (NS 716 777), was situated to the south of the Garrell Burn (**fig 15**). Roy's map of 1747–55 (**fig 5**) shows it within a large square enclosure immediately to the west of the burgh.[42] When this house was built is unknown: one source claims it was 'of date 1655' but another states it was 'built after the Restoration'. The house was 'nearly entire' in 1875, although its gardens had by then disappeared under houses for the poor.[43] The house survives, in a much-altered form, as the church hall of the later parish church. Above one of the entrances is a stone with the initials AG, referring to the former minister Archibald Graham, and 1628 inscribed upon it. The present frontage onto Church Street has doorways with channelled ashlar margins. This part of the building appears to be the remains of an eighteenth-century range which, according to the 1st Edition Ordnance Survey map of 1865, then extended further west (**fig 8**). [44]

It has been claimed that new feus were granted by James, 2nd Viscount Kilsyth in 1679, but the authors have found no supporting evidence for this. [45] Some evidence of the burgage plots, known as the 'lang rigs', which were characteristic of the period, are still visible today behind Main Street. A 'large boulder' marked on a nineteenth-century plan at the rear corner of a property in Pirnie Street may have been a boundary stone marking the southern extent of the burgh. [46]

The block between Market Square and Main Street (**fig 15**) may be a later infill of a larger market area. Part of the pattern of burgage plots still survives, especially on the west side of Main Street, although it has been much eroded by developments in the backlands and clearance for car parking. The High Street formerly extended to the south, where it forked. Much of this southern part of the town has been demolished in the twentieth century during developments in connection with the building of U P Road (after the United Presbyterian church) (**fig 15**).

FIGURE 14
Market Square, early
twentieth century
(Reproduced by permission of
North Lanarkshire Council
Museums and Heritage Service;
© North Lanarkshire Council
Museums and Heritage Service)

The date of the setting out of Market Square, to the north of Market Street, is unknown. Market Street leads in the direction of the common land in Barrwood, to the east of the town, where land was granted by the Livingstons to the feuars of the burgh in the early part of the century. Following the grant of Barrwood land, the feuars agreed by common consent on their grazing rights according to an individual's size of holding within the burgh. Those with a tenth of an acre could graze one cow; a fifth of an acre, two cows. Each feuar housed his animals in a byre on his own burgage plot. A common herdsman drove the cows each morning to the common and returned them in the evening. [47]

Building away from the Garrell and Ebroch Burns (**fig 3**) removed the new properties from an immediate water source and other solutions had to be found:

> that precious article was brought in earthen pipes, from a neighbouring spring about a quarter of a mile from the town; And a well or cistern was made near the centre of the new town, which stills bears the date 1676. Since that period, other cisterns supplied by the same spring, have been erected in other parts of the town, especially in the year 1716. [48]

The year 1676 also saw the creation of a piped water supply in Edinburgh, [49] albeit on a somewhat grander scale.

The Court House was formerly sited in the north-west corner of Market Square (**figs 14 & 15**). It had an outside stair, and underneath was the gaol, called the 'Black Hole'. The name was fitting, for the floor was damp and foul, and there was only one small stanchioned window in the north wall. [50]

The parish of Monyabroch was enlarged in 1649, when it gained the West Barony portion of neighbouring Campsie, thereby forming Kilsyth parish. [51] It appears that many residents still referred to the parish of Monyabroch as late as the mid-eighteenth century. [52] The old parish church (**fig 3**), to the south of the town, continued to serve the parish. It was altered in the early seventeenth century when the east gable was repaired and a belfry erected. A bell, dated 1626, was in use until 1823 when it cracked and had to be recast. [53] Repairs were made to the roof during the time of James Hay, minister from 1692, and the north aisle, with the burial vault of the Livingstons of Kilsyth under it, was repaired in 1697. [54] When this vault was accidentally opened, in 1795, the embalmed bodies of Jean Cochrane, the wife of William Livingston, and her son were found 'in a remarkable state of preservation'. [55] Jean Cochrane was the Viscountess of Dundee and widow of John Graham of Claverhouse, Viscount Dundee, who was killed leading the Jacobites to victory at Killiecrankie in 1689. The lady and her child had been killed at Utrecht in 1695, when the roof of their lodging had collapsed (**fig 21**). [56]

The internal arrangement of the old parish church is described by Anderson:

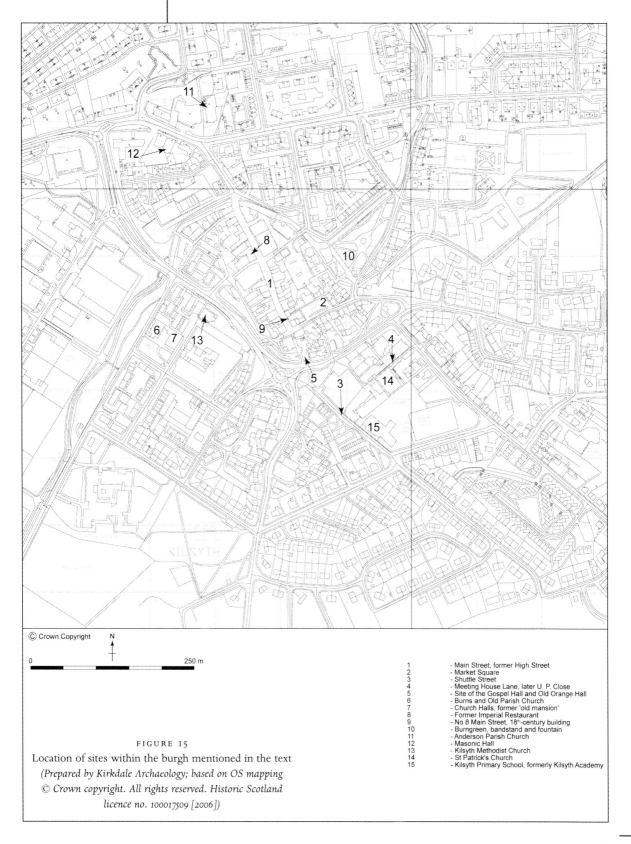

N

0   250 m

1	- Main Street, former High Street
2	- Market Square
3	- Shuttle Street
4	- Meeting House Lane, later U. P. Close
5	- Site of the Gospel Hall and Old Orange Hall
6	- Burns and Old Parish Church
7	- Church Halls, former 'old mansion'
8	- Former Imperial Restaurant
9	- No 8 Main Street, 18th-century building
10	- Burngreen, bandstand and fountain
11	- Anderson Parish Church
12	- Masonic Hall
13	- Kilsyth Methodist Church
14	- St Patrick's Church
15	- Kilsyth Primary School, formerly Kilsyth Academy

FIGURE 15

Location of sites within the burgh mentioned in the text

(Prepared by Kirkdale Archaeology; based on OS mapping
© Crown copyright. All rights reserved. Historic Scotland
licence no. 100017509 [2006])

The old church was barn-like in shape. There was a small belfry on the top of the East gable, from which the bell-rope hung down outside the wall. The main door was in the centre of the South wall, and the people entering in at it passed under the pulpit to the right and left, into the area of the church. The table seats were in a line from the pulpit to the North wall. At the East end of that North wall there was an aisle, reserved in the olden time for the gentry. The Livingston vault was there. There were three lofts or galleries. The one to the East, or right hand of the pulpit, was called the bell-loft, because of the bell on that gable. The loft in front of the pulpit was called the aisle loft, because of the aisle below it; the gallery or loft to the West, or left hand of the pulpit, was called the Moorland and Banton loft. Each of these galleries had an outside door to the gallery stair, one of which gallery doors was in the North wall. The aisle had an entry to itself, also to the North. There were five outside doors altogether, three being in the South wall, and two in the North one. The church had accommodation for six hundred sitters.[57]

The group of buildings around Garrell Mill (**fig 3**) are of late seventeenth-century date. Garrell Mill House (NS 7200 7831; Category B-listed) consists of a two-storey range including cottage and coach house. There is a cubical sundial on the south corner. Garrell Mill (NS 7201 7831; Category B-listed), on the opposite side of the road from the Mill House, has twin stone gables with wagon entrances. There is a stone dated 1700 inset above the keystone of one of the wagon entrances. Two other stones carry the dates 1774 and 1808.[58] A testament by John Napier, under-miller at 'Gorbalmill, parish of Kilsyth' is dated 1671 and demonstrates the earlier origins of the mill.[59]

The eighteenth century

The early eighteenth century saw a change in landownership. In 1715, the Livingstons of Kilsyth were forfeited for their part in the failed Jacobite rising of that year. The estates were subsequently managed by the York Building Company. A survey of the estate in 1716 recorded that there was 'a pretty Good little house Called the House of Killsyth with Gardins and Severall very large Parks of Inclosures, and a Dove house and There is another very old Ruinous house a short way from Killsyth Call the Coll[i]um'. If the survey was comprehensive, then it would appear that there were 49 property-holders in the town of Kilsyth who held their feus from the former viscounts.[60]

When the York Building Company went bankrupt, the Kilsyth lands came into the hands of a 'Mr Campbell of Shawfield', Glasgow.[61] They were then bought by Sir Archibald Edmonstone of Duntreath in 1783, who built Colzium House (NS 7288 7866; Category B-listed) near the site of the earlier castle, which had been demolished in 1703. The house was extended in 1861, but by the 1920s, the Edmonstones were selling off their lands.[62] In 1937, the house, its grounds, and its policies were bequeathed to the people of Kilsyth by the town's former clerk, William MacKay Lennox.[63]

During the mid-eighteenth century, Kilsyth became the well-known centre of a religious revival. In 1742, after nearly three decades as Kilsyth's minister, Mr James Robe witnessed what he deemed to be 'the Extraordinary work of the Spirit of God' in that community. It was his opinion that there were about 'eleven hundred examinable persons' (adults able to take communion) at that time. It seems that although formerly the Kilsyth population had been inclined towards 'sitting idle at their doors, and strolling in the streets profanely upon the Lord's day', Robe's preaching had, by the 1740s, given them 'a discreet and towardly disposition'.[64] Some, it seems, were less convinced by Robe's abilities. His claim that the presence of the Holy Spirit had induced fainting was dismissed by his critics as epileptic fits.[65]

The layout of the town at this period can be seen in William Roy's *Military Survey* map of 1747–55 (**fig 5**).[66] The north–south line of High Street, forking at its southern end, is clearly shown. Adjoining it to the west is the large enclosure of the former mansion house. The partly ruinous house itself was occupied by the minister, Mr James Robe. Later, in the early nineteenth century, the premises were used as a tambouring school by a Mrs Lamont, who taught young people to embroider fine muslin there. The building survived multiple occupancies in the early twentieth century and is now in commercial use as the Church Street Halls.[67]

Kilsyth benefited from being on the Edinburgh to Glasgow road, which passed to the north of the town and was served by the Duntreath Arms Inn (**fig 3**). New housing is being built on the site (NS 719 781) but the boundary walls still survive. The road system was improved in the mid-eighteenth century. Following an Act of 1752, a turnpike road was built between Kirkintilloch and Falkirk.[68] A route map of 1776 (**fig 6**) showing the road from Stirling to Glasgow clearly shows Kilsyth and its toll point.[69] The road from the east approached the town along the present Coach Road and entered the town along Market Street. The traveller would then turn north along High Street (the present Main Street) to the line of the present Glasgow Road, where a toll would be paid before continuing westwards. The opening of the turnpike road to Kirkintilloch was an important step in the movement of the main east–west road to the north of the old burgh, which eventually led to the focus of the settlement shifting away from the historic core. The prosperity of the burgh was handicapped by the opening of a new route from Glasgow to Edinburgh via Cumbernauld in the early 1790s, which diverted trade from the town.[70] The minister of Kilsyth commented in 1841 that:

> About half a century ago, it was the great thoroughfare betwixt the
> metropolis and Glasgow. Now, it is rare to see any vehicle on the

MAIN ST. FROM NEAR RAILWAY BRIDGE KILSYTH

streets, superior to a cart or the post gig. There is not even one post-chaise, but very comfortable accommodation in the chief inn, for families travelling in their own vehicles.[71]

The loss of road traffic was partly compensated for by the building of the Forth & Clyde Canal (**fig 3**) so that, in 1841, it could be said that 'the canal is our principal mode of communication with other parts of the country'.[72] The section to the south of Kilsyth was constructed in 1770 although the whole canal was not completed until 1790.[73] Both freight and passenger services operated from the basin at Auchinstarry, the latter connecting with coach services at points along the canal. The building of the canal also stimulated the local industries, especially quarrying. Situated close to the canal, the Auchinstarry quarry (NS 7205 7714) (**fig 3**) provided a huge source of whinstone used for setts and paving, especially for the Glasgow building industry.

The building of the canal brought another change to the local landscape with the creation of a reservoir (NS 7339 7855 to NS 7446 7872), 2 km to the north-east of Kilsyth, to supply water to the canal. It was created in 1771–73 by flooding the valley of the Banton Burn (site of the Battle of Kilsyth) and was fed partly by a lade (NS 7200 7842 to NS 7339 7855) from the diverted Garrell Burn at Garrell Mill (**fig 3**).[74] This greatly reduced the volume of

FIGURE 16
Main Street from the railway bridge, c 1900
(Reproduced by permission of North Lanarkshire Council Museums and Heritage Service; © North Lanarkshire Council Museums and Heritage Service)

water flowing past Kilsyth, which could explain the ruined waulk mill near the confluence of the Garrell Burn and the Ebroch Burn, shown on a map of 1764 depicting the proposed route of the canal.[75]

Most of the buildings that had survived from the eighteenth century into the present were, unfortunately, demolished in the late twentieth century, with the exception of *nos* 48 and 50 Market Street. They date from the late eighteenth century and form a two-storey building with unevenly spaced windows and a nepus gable (Category C(S)-listed).

The former Orange Lodge at *no* 11 High Street, which was demolished in 1985, probably dated from the eighteenth century (**fig 10**), as did its neighbour, the former Gospel Hall, at *no* 3 Market Close, which once displayed a date panel marked 1764 (**fig 11**); it has also been demolished.[76] The Lodge had windows with raised margins and a projecting eaves course. A panel was set below the central window on the third storey; this featured a cordiner's crown and rounding-knife, which divided the initials WH and the date 1765 (**fig 12**).[77] It has been surmised that WH stood for William Hamilton, a shoemaker who sold the upper part of the property to the masons in 1769.[78] The house was examined in 1978, when it was noted that the ground floor dated from 1679 and contained a corbelled lintel fireplace of that period.[79]

The adjacent Gospel Hall, like the Orange Lodge, was demolished in 1985 (**fig 10**). Previously thought to date from the early nineteenth century, this much-altered structure had been built of squared-off coursed stone rubble. It was reduced in height and a moulded cornice added to its front façade later in its life. A carved panel dated 1764 was set into the façade depicting a man in a skirted coat between the initials J H and H [?K] and the motto RENOVATE AN[IMAS] (Renew your spirits) (**fig 11**).[80] The panel was thought to have been re-used from an earlier building, but a re-examination of the evidence suggests that the building was probably older than the Orange Lodge and may date from the earliest days of the burgh. Prior to demolition, the Orange Lodge had been given a Category B listing and the Gospel Hall had been a Category C(S)-listed building.

The water supply to the burgh was supplemented in the late eighteenth century when the springs on the slopes above Kilsyth were presented to the town by Sir Archibald Edmonstone, together with £100 to bring the water in.[81]

The old parish church to the south of the town continued in use during the eighteenth century. A new manse (NS 7183 7721) (**fig 8**) was erected in 1786, across the road to the east of the church. Later extended, the manse was still standing in 1918 but has subsequently been demolished.[82] The glebe land had not been enclosed as late as 1797, although the authors of the *New Statistical Account* thought this development to be imminent; instead, it stood in 'a variety of lots'.[83]

In 1750, the common land of Barrwood (**figs 3 & 8**) was enclosed into three equal portions to facilitate arable cultivation. Following a dispute in 1808 among the feuars over rights of common pasture, the enclosed land began to be divided up into individual small raised plots known as lazybeds. This land subsequently became known as the Couches.[84] The pattern of small rectangular plots established at this time survives in the area of Mid Barrwood, *c* 1 km east of the burgh (NS 727 778).[85]

The nineteenth century

In 1826, Kilsyth's charter of 1620, erecting it as a burgh of barony, was renewed. This enabled the election of a bailie, a dean of guild for the adjustment of weights and measures, a treasurer, and four councillors. They also gained a clerk and a procurator-fiscal. In addition, the town was given the right to hold a weekly market and two annual fairs.[86] In 1840, Kilsyth adopted the Burgh Police (Scotland) Act of 1833 to enable the imposition of a rate for paving, lighting, and water. It is reputed that a hiatus in the burgh's government around this time was finally resolved in 1878, when a new administration comprised of nine individuals was elected under the Burgh Police (Scotland) Act.[87]

These changes were expressed in the development of new civic buildings in the Market Square. The Market Chambers (**fig 13**) at *nos* 6–10 Market Street (Category B-listed) were constructed in 1860 on the site of the old barony court house. They have four raised gothic gabled dormers and ground-floor openings with dripstones. On the east side of Market Square was a two-storey building (**fig 14**) which had formerly been an inn. It had an extruded semicircular staircase tower to the rear, with a substantial central newel, giving access to the upper apartments. This building was demolished in 1978.[88]

Much of Main Street was rebuilt during the late nineteenth century (**figs 16 & 18**). At *no* 11 Main Street, the gable-roofed building displays the date 1869 and *no* 14 is dated 1882. The property at *nos* 36–42 Main Street, once occupied by 'The White House, Outfitters and Clothiers', appears to be of the late nineteenth century, although the date 1910 is displayed on the chimney of the nepus gable (**fig 17**). It is currently in poor condition but retains original high-quality shopfronts (NS 7178 7786; Category B-listed), each of three bays with a central recessed door, large glass panes (now boarded), and original timber fascia boards.

The early nineteenth century saw a planned expansion of Kilsyth in the lands of the 'old mansion' to the west of the burgh, where a 'new town' was created (**fig 22**). This was intended to accommodate a growing population, which had reached 4297 in 1831.[89] New feus for the scheme were granted in the late 1780s by Sir Archibald Edmonstone of Duntreath with the purpose of

FIGURE 17
The White House, *no* 38
Main Street, 1988
(By courtesy of RCAHMS;
© Crown copyright RCAHMS)

creating 'a complete new town'.[90] It was laid out along Newtown Street and crossed by Church Street. West Port Street, now partly renamed as an extension of Market Street and Park Lane, was also incorporated. The original houses have gone, but the street pattern still survives.

The building of a new parish church (**figs 15 & 19**) was an integral part of this residential redevelopment. The old parish church was replaced in 1816 by a new building with 860 sittings in Backbrae Street, which is now known as the Burns and Old Parish Church (NS 7168 7781; Category B-listed).[91] It is distinguished by a buttressed gothic nave with raised pointed finials and a battlemented tower; the chancel is a later addition. The graveyard of the former parish church continued to be used; it contains many tombstones dating from the seventeenth and eighteenth centuries, some of which display emblems depicting the occupation of the deceased (**fig 20**).[92] The graveyard entrance has rusticated gate piers with ball finials and in the corner of the graveyard there is an octagonal watch-house (Category B-listed), built in 1816 to guard against the activities of body-snatchers (**fig 21**).[93] The cemetery was extended to the west in 1908.[94]

FIGURE 18
Main Street, 1980
(By courtesy of RCAHMS;
© Crown copyright RCAHMS)

A number of other churches were erected within the burgh during the nineteenth century, reflecting the diverse religious life of the community. The Methodist church in Church Street was completed in 1884 and opened its doors in 1885.[95] The Anderson United Presbyterian Church, now Anderson parish church (**fig 15**), was built in 1893 to replace the building near Shuttle Street that had given rise to the name of U P Road.[96] The Masonic Hall (**fig 15**) in Parkfoot Street opened in 1901.[97]

The mid-nineteenth century saw greater concerns for public health, resulting in improved housing and sanitation. It was noted in 1845 that 'the streets have been very much improved of late by levelling, removal of out-stairs, and nuisances'.[98] Despite these developments, 35 persons were to die in Kilsyth during the cholera epidemic of 1849. A pump (Category C(S)-listed) was installed in Market Square in 1869 by Sir Archibald Edmonstone (**figs 13 & 14**). F H Groome, in his *Ordnance Gazetteer* of 1883, mentions 'a new drainage system, effected at a cost of £2250'.[99] Other improvements in public utilities included the provision of gas; the Kilsyth Gas Company was established in 1835.[100] Its works were situated to the north of the Garrell Burn (NS 7160 7800) (**fig 9**).

The predominant trade in Kilsyth during the early nineteenth century was hand-loom weaving for Glasgow manufacturers. This legacy is preserved in the name Shuttle Street, which was formerly lined with weavers' cottages.[101] Two textile factories were established in the town. Wilson's factory (NS 716 778), formerly in Backbrae Street, employed 50 weavers who produced mainly coarse lappets. A waulking factory, for finishing cloth, operated at Quinzie Mill.[102] The land alongside the Garrell Burn, on the west side of Backbrae Street, was used as a bleaching green.[103] During the first half of the nineteenth century, hand-loom weavers found it increasingly difficult to compete with larger enterprises investing in power looms. Wages and living standards declined and weavers found themselves at the mercy of their agents, who reduced the local weaving rates by 25 per cent.[104] The situation reached a

FIGURE 19
Parish church from Backbrae Street, 1959 *(By courtesy of RCAHMS; © Crown copyright RCAHMS)*

crisis in 1826, when 1400 of Kilsyth's 1500 weavers were unemployed (the total population then being about 4260). Free meals were distributed to the poorest families and others were encouraged to seek alternative employment in the quarries or on the roads.[105] There was little improvement in the following years: Kilsyth's specialised embroiderers of fine muslin, called tambourers, were said to be in a 'most depressed condition' in 1841.[106]

The improvements in transport brought about an increase in coal-mining. Baird & Company opened a number of coal and ironstone mines in the

FIGURE 21
Watch-house with Jean
Cochrane's memorial,
Kilsyth cemetery, 2004
(Photo: L Stewart)

Kilsyth area, necessitating the recruitment of labour from Ireland.[107] Miners' rows, such as the former Kingston Rows (NS 717 782) shown on the Ordnance Survey map of 1865 (**fig 8**),[108] were built to the north of the town, near the collieries.

The railway (**figs 3 & 9**) came late to Kilsyth, although a line had been planned from 1845.[109] The Kelvin Valley Railway, linking Kilsyth with the North British Railway line at Lenzie, was opened for passengers and freight on 1 June 1878.[110] By 1882, the Kilsyth and Bonnybridge Railway Company had come into existence. Construction of a line linking Kilsyth to the existing North British Railway network was undertaken by Messrs James Young and

Company of Dixon Street, Glasgow.[111] The line opened in 1888,[112] whereupon a station master, Mr L Crombie, was hired at £85 per annum.[113] Kilsyth's railway link was closed in the 1960s and is now a footpath to Colzium.[114]

The twentieth century

While the population of Kilsyth remained constant through the first half of the twentieth century, being 11,052 in 1901 and 11,990 in 1951,[115] there was a move away from the centre of the old burgh to the peripheral areas. After 1950, new roads were created and properties were cleared from the backlands of the old burgage plots, initially to improve sanitation but latterly, to facilitate car parking and service access. An account of the parish in 1966 noted that 'like many other places in Scotland, Kilsyth has pulled down its back wynd,'[116] in order to create space for car parks. There was an increase in housing outside the historic core of Kilsyth. Attractive Edwardian villas still surround Burngreen (**fig 15**), which was landscaped in 1910 to create a formal garden (NS 7192 7792). It features an ornamental bandstand (**fig 23**), a cast-iron fountain surmounted with a Grecian maiden, iron railings, and bridged walkways. Housing was constructed after the First World War on Kelvin Way and Kingsway. There was a further expansion of housing in the 1970s to the north-west of the town along the lower slopes of the Kilsyth Hills, with more recent building in the area of Garrell Mill, to the north-east of the town (**fig 3**).

Several notable public buildings were erected in Kilsyth during the twentieth century. A new Kilsyth Academy (NS 7123 7825) was designed in the 1930s by the eminent architect Sir Basil Spence and opened in 1954.[117] This building, 'gaunt in its extremely modern architecture',[118] occupies a dominant position on the north side of the town. The elegant former Academy in Shuttle Street (**figs 9, 15 & 24**) was built in 1876 but has mostly been demolished; an early twentieth-century extension now houses the primary school.

Main Street was enhanced in 1904–05 by the erection of the three-storey red ashlar shop and tenement, the former Imperial Restaurant, at *nos* 55–63 Main Street (**fig 15**), designed by George Hay (NS 7175 7790; Category B-listed). The building, which displays the influence of the Glasgow Style, has alternate splayed bays in cavetto recesses through its upper two storeys. The cornices at first-floor level have a sinuous keyblock treatment and the parapets have curved tops. The overall fascia of the original shopfront survives; there is some engraved glass and doors with onion shaped fanlights. The interior of *no* 55 Main Street, now a general store, had until recently retained the original woodwork screens, stained glass, and light fittings of the former Imperial Restaurant.

Religion continued to play an important part in Kilsyth life into the twentieth century. One local writer noted that 'reverence for the Church and

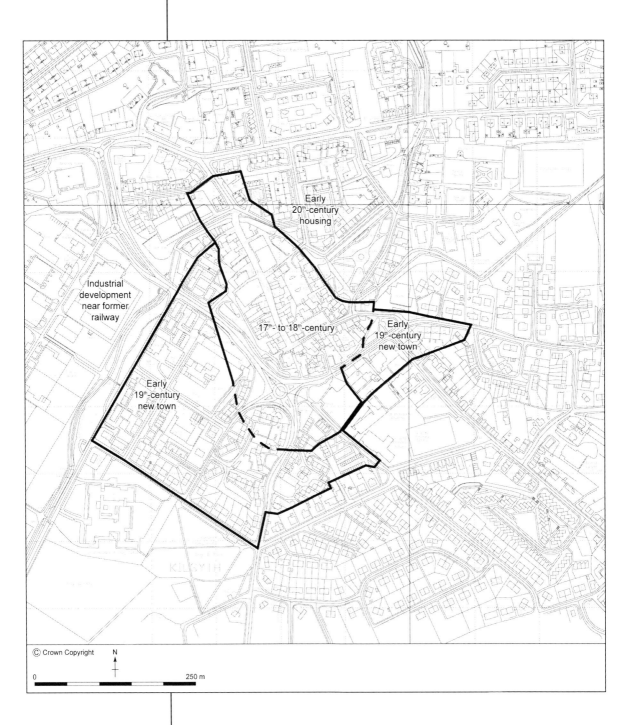

Early
20th-century
housing

Industrial
development
near former
railway

17th- to 18th-century

Early
19th-century
new town

Early
19th-century
new town

© Crown Copyright

N

0   250 m

clergy' was still 'in full flower' in 1960s' Kilsyth, particularly amongst the town's women.[119] The church was especially active in promoting temperance in the town and Kilsyth officially became 'dry' in 1920 – this would have pleased the writer of the *New Statistical Account*, who complained in 1845 that there were as many as 22 premises selling alcohol in the town! It was not until 1967 that Kilsyth's inhabitants decided to allow the sale and purchase of

FIGURE 23
Burngreen bandstand, 2003
(Photo: D Gallagher)

alcohol again.[120] A new church called the 'Church of God' was founded in 1902 by local pit manager William Irvine. In 1905, the evangelical Irish preacher Edward Cooney was invited to Kilsyth by Irvine, whereupon nineteen people were baptised by immersion in Banton Loch.[121]

In the mid-twentieth century, it was estimated that a quarter of Kilsyth's population was Roman Catholic.[122] St Patrick's Roman Catholic church (NS 7197 7771; Category A-listed) (**fig 15**) at *no 30* Low Craigends was built in 1964 to replace an older building. The new building was designed by the architects Gillespie, Kidd & Coia. It has a rectangular plan and is constructed of red brick with a flat steel-truss roof, copper clad, with deep eaves projecting at 45 degrees.[123]

During the mid-twentieth century Kilsyth was the home of Scotland's only coffin furnishers, Murdoch & Company. Their factory on Parkfoot Street, which sent coffin fittings across the globe to the Commonwealth nations, was once Kilsyth's largest employer; in 1966, there were still 200 persons on the payroll. The factory has since been demolished to make way for housing.[124]

Significant changes to the street layout in Kilsyth have occurred during the second half of the twentieth century. The creation of residential areas at Westfield and Balmalloch to the north and at Barrwood to the south has led to the building of new roads through the town. Airdrie Road and U P Road, to the immediate south-west of the historic core of the burgh, dislocated the old centre from its surroundings. A Conservation Area was designated in 1974 and modified in March 1984. At present it embraces both the old town centre and Burngreen.[125]

Kilsyth's convenient situation on the Glasgow–Edinburgh route, close to a good water supply, has ensured continuous human activity in the area for many centuries. From its seventeenth-century origins as a small market centre, Kilsyth expanded during the late eighteenth and early nineteenth centuries, as weaving, coal-mining, and quarrying changed the economic function of the town. Over the past century, however, the historic core has become obscured by unsympathetic redevelopment. It is hoped that this survey may help to promote a greater awareness both of Kilsyth's archaeological potential and the need for greater investment in its existing architectural heritage.

Notes

1. A S Henshall, *The Chambered Tombs of Scotland* (Edinburgh, 1963), ii, 492–3; RCAHMS, *Stirlingshire: An Inventory of the Ancient Monuments* (Edinburgh, 1963), 64

2. J Anderson and G F Black, 'Reports on local museums in Scotland', *Proc Soc Antiq Scot*, 22 (1887–88), 349

3. W L Philips, P Philips and J G Scott, 'Croy, stone axehead', *DES* (1973), 24–5

4. *OSA*, ix, 408, 488, 489

5. J M Coles, 'Scottish Middle Bronze Age metalwork, *Proc Soc Antiq Scot*, 97 (1963–64), 135

6. J M Coles, 'Scottish Late Bronze Age metalwork: typology, distribution and chronology', *Proc Soc Antiq Scot*, 93 (1959–60), 68

7. D J Breeze, *The Northern Frontiers of Roman Britain* (London, 1982), 29–30

8. A Gordon, *Itinerarium Septentrionale, or a Journey Thro' Most of the Counties of Scotland and those in the North of England* (London, 1726), 21; RCAHMS, *Stirlingshire* (1963), 84–5; RCAHMS, *The Archaeological Sites and Monuments of Cumbernauld and Kilsyth District and Strathkelvin District, Strathclyde Region* (Edinburgh, 1982), 8

9. RCAHMS, *Stirlingshire*, 173–4; RCAHMS, *Cumbernauld and Kilsyth* (1982), 10; L Keppie, 'A Roman Altar from Kilsyth', *Glasgow Archaeological Journal*, 5 (1978), 19–24

10. *OSA*, ix, 485

11. RCAHMS, *Stirlingshire*, 84; RCAHMS, *Cumbernauld and Kilsyth* (1982), 7

12. I Fisher, 'The Early Christian Period in Stirling and Central Scotland' in J Gifford and F A Walker, *Stirling and Central Scotland* (Edinburgh, 2002), 15–16

13. RCAHMS, *Cumbernauld and Kilsyth* (1982), 10

14. H B Millar, *History of Cumbernauld and Kilsyth from earliest times: including a guide to places of interest in the district* (Cumbernauld, 1980), 11

15. *OSA*, ix, 422; RCAHMS, *Stirlingshire*, 435

16. *OSA*, ix, 422

17. *Origines Parochiales Scotiae: The Antiquities Ecclesiastical and Territorial of the Parishes of Scotland* (Bannatyne Club, 1851–55), i, 43

18. *Handlist of the Acts of Alexander II*, J M Scoular (ed) (1959), no 347

19. *Handlist of the Acts of Alexander III, The Guardians, John, 1249–1296*, G G Simpson (ed) (1960), no 7

20. *The Scots Peerage*, ed. J Balfour-Paul (Edinburgh, 1904–14), v, 183; *RMS*, vi, 312

21. *Scots Peerage*, v, 184–5, 425

22. W D Simpson, 'Notes on Lulach's Stone, Kildrummy, Aberdeenshire: A Symbol Stone recently found in Mortlach Churchyard, Banffshire; and other antiquities', *Proc Soc Antiq Scot*, 60 (1925–26), 280; RCAHMS, *The Archaeological Sites and Monuments of Cumbernauld and Kilsyth District and Strathkelvin District, Strathclyde Region* (1978), 15–16

23. Millar, *Cumbernauld and Kilsyth*, 15; P Anton, *Kilsyth: A Parish History* (Glasgow, 1893), 180–1; RCAHMS, *Cumbernauld and Kilsyth* (1978), 25

24. H B Millar, 'Kilsyth Castle', *DES* (1976), 64

25. NLS, Adv MS 70.2.9 (Pont 32)

26. M Ponsford, 'Post-Medieval Britain and Ireland in 2002', *Post-Medieval Archaeology*, 37.2 (2003), 351

27. D MacGibbon and T Ross, *The Castellated and Domestic Architecture of Scotland from the Twelfth to the Eighteenth Centuries* (Edinburgh 1887–92), iii, 474; N Tranter, *The Fortified House in Scotland* (Edinburgh and London, 1962–70), iii, 153; RCAHMS, *Cumbernauld and Kilsyth* (1982), 21

28. Ponsford, 'Post-Medieval Britain', 351; NLS, Adv Ms 70.2.9 (Pont 32); NLS, Adv Ms 70.2.10 (Gordon 50); NLS, EMS. b. 2.1(19), H Moll, 'The Shires of Stirling and Clackmannan' (1745); NLS, EMS. s. 623, J Grassom, 'County of Stirling'; NLS, EMS. s. 712(14), Thomson, 'Stirlingshire'

29. H B Millar, 'Kilsyth burgh, farm-house, medieval artefacts', *DES* (1979), 34

30. NLS, Adv MS 70.2.9 (Pont 32)

31. RCAHMS, *Cumbernauld and Kilsyth*, (1978), 15

32. I B Cowan, *The Parishes of Medieval Scotland* (Edinburgh, 1967), 150

33. J Kirk, *The Books of Assumptions of the Thirds of Benefices. Scottish Ecclesiastical Rentals at the Reformation* (Oxford, 1995), 506

34. *RMS*, viii, 25–6; G S Pryde, *The Burghs of Scotland: A Critical List* (London, 1965), 67; Millar, *Cumbernauld and Kilsyth*, 61

35. *OSA*, ix, 438

36. H B Millar, 'Kilsyth and the Couches' (Cumbernauld and Kilsyth Museums Information Sheet. Cumbernauld, nd), 1

37. *OSA*, ix, 439 This may be a premature assumption on the part of the writer, as several seventeenth-century maps still refer to Burnside. It may only have acquired the name Kilsyth in the eighteenth or early nineteenth century. NLS, EMS. s. 623, Grassom, 'County of Stirling'

38. *NSA*, viii, 148

39. NLS, EMS. s. 712(14), J Ainslie, 'Map of the Southern Part of Scotland, 1821'

40. Sir James was made Viscount of Kilsyth and Lord Campsie by Charles II in 1661, *Scots Peerage*, v, 191–2; *APS*, vii, 315

41. *APS*, vii, 315; J Nicoll, *A Diary of Public Transactions and other Occurrences chiefly in Scotland, from January 1650 to June 1667*, D Laing (ed) (Bannatyne Club, 1836), 134

42. W Roy, *The Military Antiquities of the Romans in Britain* (London, 1793), no XXXV

43. *NSA*, viii, 148; A Edmonstone, *Genealogical Account of the Family of Edmonstone*

of Duntreath (Edinburgh, 1875), 11

44. 'Stirlingshire', Ordnance Survey, 1st edn, 1:10,560 scale (sheet XXVIII, 1865)

45. Millar, *Cumbernauld and Kilsyth*, 61–2 Millar's map has no references and efforts by the authors to locate any source on which it was based have been unsuccessful. Millar, 'Kilsyth and the Couches', 1–2

46. NAS, RHP 82530, Architectural block plan of subjects in Shuttle Street and Pirnie Street, Kilsyth (nd)

47. Millar, 'Kilsyth and the Couches', 2–3

48. Millar, 'Kilsyth and the Couches', 1

49. RCAHMS, *An Inventory of the Ancient and Historical Monuments of the City of Edinburgh* (Edinburgh, 1951), lxxi

50. R A Anderson, *A History of Kilsyth and A Memorial of Two Lives: 1793–1901* (Kilsyth, Edinburgh and Glasgow, 1901), 126

51. *Ordnance Gazetteer of Scotland*, F H Groome (ed) (Edinburgh, 1883), iv, 386

52. *NSA*, viii, 138

53. *OSA*, ix, 438; R W M Clouston, 'The Church and Other Bells of Stirlingshire', *Proc Soc Antiq Scot*, 84 (1949–50), 80

54. *OSA*, ix, 441

55. Anton, *Kilsyth*, 55; J F and S Mitchell, *Monumental Inscriptions (pre-1855) in West Stirlingshire* (Edinburgh, 1970), 152

56. *Scots Peerage*, v, 193

57. Anderson, *History of Kilsyth*, 11–12

58. J R Hume, *The Industrial Archaeology of Scotland, 1: Lowlands and Borders* (London, 1976), 253

59. NAS, CC9/7/1671, Testament of John Napier

60. NAS, CS129–63, Acts of Sequestration, Kilsyth Estate, 10 July 1716; NAS, E640/1, Rental of the Estate, 1716–19

61. Millar, *Cumbernauld and Kilsyth*, 32; Edmonstone, *Genealogical Account*, 11

62. Millar, *Cumbernauld and Kilsyth*, 66; *Third Stat Acc*, xviii, 274

63. *Third Stat Acc*, xviii, 273

64. J Robe, *Narratives of the Extraordinary Work of the Spirit of God at Cambuslang, Kilsyth, etc begun 1742* (1790), 64

65. Robe, *Narratives*, 179

66. W Roy, *Military Survey of Scotland, 1747–55*, BL, C9b5

67. J Gordon, *Kilsyth History Trail* (Kilsyth, 1980), 4

68. R Smith, *The Making of Scotland* (Edinburgh, 2001), 525

69. NLS, Taylor and Skinner, *A General Map of the Roads, made out of Actual Surveys taken out by Geo Taylor and Andrew Skinner* (London, 1776)

70. *OSA, ix, 505*

71. *NSA*, viii, 159

72. *NSA*, 160

73. NAS, FCN/1/1, Records of the British Railways Board, Forth & Clyde Canal, Minute Book, 1767–70

74. J Lindsay, *The Canals of Scotland* (Newton Abbot, 1968), 24–5; RCAHMS, *Stirlingshire*, 437

75. J Smeaton, *Plan of the Tract of Country between the Forth and Clyde with proposals*

for a canal, Royal Society Archives JS/6/64. Microfilm copy in the NMRS.

76. Information supplied by Mr John Gordon, Kilsyth Academy
77. RCAHMS, *Stirlingshire*, 312
78. Information care of Mr John Gordon, now in Kilsyth Library
79. Millar, *Cumbernauld and Kilsyth*, 63
80. *Ibid*
81. T Robertson and D Haldane, *The Economic Geology of the Central Coalfield. Area 1 Kilsyth and Kirkintilloch*, (Edinburgh, 1937), 155
82. 'Stirlingshire', Ordnance Survey, 2nd edn, 1:2500 scale (sheet XXVIII, 1898)
83. *NSA*, viii, 445
84. Millar, 'Kilsyth and the Couches', 3–4; NAS, RHP, 46700, Plan of the Estate of Kilsyth, the property of Sir Archibald Edmonstone, adjoining the town of Kilsyth, 1856. The area is marked as 'Common' on this map.
85. Gordon, *Kilsyth History Trail*, 7
86. R Handyside, 'Report on the Burgh and Barony of Kilsyth', *Reports of Commissioners on Municipal Corporations, Scotland* (London, 1836), 651
87. *Third Stat Acc*, xviii, 275
88. NMRS, STR/13/1; Details from Mr John Gordon
89. Handyside, 'Report on the Burgh and Barony of Kilsyth', 651
90. *OSA*, ix, 506–07
91. Groome, *Ordnance Gazetteer*, 386
92. Mitchell and Mitchell, *Monumental Inscriptions*, 149–76
93. Gordon, *Kilsyth History Trail*, 6
94. NAS, RHP 82505, Plan showing ground to be acquired for extension of cemetery, 1908
95. Gordon, *Kilsyth History Trail*, 4
96. Gordon, *Kilsyth History Trail*, 3
97. *Ibid*
98. *NSA*, viii, 168
99. Groome, *Ordnance Gazetteer*, 386
100. Gordon, *Kilsyth History Trail*, 3–4
101. Gordon, *Kilsyth History Trail*, 3
102. *NSA*, viii, 159; Gordon, *Kilsyth History Trail*, 4
103. Pencil annotation, NAS, RHP 46700, Plan of part of the estate of Kilsyth adjoining the town of Kilsyth, 1856
104. N Murray, *The Scottish Hand Loom Weavers 1790–1850: A Social History* (Edinburgh, 1978), 70
105. Questionnaire issued by the Edinburgh Committee for the Relief of the Unemployed Manufacturers in Scotland, 1826, Glasgow University Library, Eph L/169 (SCRAN 000–000–576–387-C)
106. *NSA*, viii, 160
107. A B Campbell, *The Lanarkshire Miners: A Social History of their Trade Unions 1775–1875* (Edinburgh, 1979), 237
108. 'Stirlingshire', Ordnance Survey, 1st edn, 1:10,560 scale (1865)
109. NAS, RHP 85407, Plan of proposed railway from Kirkintilloch to Kilsyth, 1845

110. J Thomas, *A Regional History of the Railways of Great Britain, 6: Scotland The Lowlands and the Borders* (Newton Abbot, 1971), 81

111. NAS, BR/KBR, Kilsyth and Bonnybridge Railway Company, 1883–1923, 28 April 1886

112. Thomas, *Regional History of the Railways*, 83

113. NAS, BR/KBR, Kilsyth and Bonnybridge, 19 July 1888

114. Millar, *Cumbernauld and Kilsyth*, 35

115. *Third Stat Acc*, xviii, 273

116. *Third Stat Acc*, xviii, 290

117. NMRS, SGF/1930/3, Spence, Glover & Ferguson Collection, Kilsyth Academy, Secondary School

118. *Third Stat Acc*, xviii, 284

119. *Third Stat Acc*, xviii, 274

120. *NSA*, viii, 167; *Third Stat Acc*, xviii, 275; Details from Mr John Gordon

121. *Kilsyth Chronicle*, 5 May 1905; Correspondence with Mr John Gordon

122. *Third Stat Acc*, xviii, 273

123. R W K C Rogerson, *Jack Coia: His Life and Work* (Glasgow, 1986), 79–80

124. *Third Stat Acc*, xviii, 281; W Chalmers, *Old Kilsyth* (Ochiltree, 1997), 4–5, 10

125. North Lanarkshire Council, 'Kilsyth Conservation Area Appraisal: 31/03/2003'; Millar, *Cumbernauld and Kilsyth*, 63

4   The archaeological potential of Kilsyth

The immediate vicinity of Kilsyth contains the Antonine Wall and the Forth & Clyde Canal – archaeological landscapes of international importance. However, this rich local heritage has tended to overshadow the potential of Kilsyth as a historic burgh.[1] One aim of the final draft of the *Kilsyth Local Plan*, published in 1996, was to 'safeguard and enhance the heritage of the built environment'. It noted the character of the old town and that within the Kilsyth Conservation Area, which includes the adjacent Burngreen, there were 'many interesting nineteenth-century buildings' as well as a number of listed buildings.[2] There was no consideration, however, of the potential for buried archaeological deposits within the burgh (**fig 25**).

The most immediately accessible part of the historic environment of Kilsyth, and one that has suffered from neglect in recent years, is that of standing buildings. The change in shopping patterns in the Kilsyth area has meant that the shops in Main Street now serve a very localised catchment area and the street no longer acts as a meeting place for the local community.[3] This has resulted in a decline in the upkeep of properties and a subsequent threat to the built environment. This is exemplified by *nos* 44–48 Main Street, which have been placed on the *Buildings at Risk Register for Scotland*.[4] Kilsyth has a rich variety of buildings that encapsulate its history and provide a heritage resource that reflects the past lives of the townsfolk of Kilsyth. Some buildings have changed over time; their present exteriors can at times hide the archaeological potential of their building history. The original age of buildings can often be disguised by later alterations, such as the alteration of windows or the removal of forestairs. These buildings, fronting the street at the narrow end of the burgage plots, can encapsulate the changing history of the burgh. Recording of the archaeology of the standing structures can enhance awareness of the burgh's built heritage and aid the preservation of the historic townscape.

One objective of archaeological and historical research within Kilsyth is a better understanding of the origins of the burgh, its nature and subsequent development. Recent excavations in comparable burghs have shown that street frontages are normally the most rewarding to investigate and that evidence of earlier occupation may survive sealed beneath the eighteenth- or nineteenth-century standing buildings. There has been little archaeological investigation within Kilsyth but an excavation prior to redevelopment on the south-east corner of High Street and Market Street (NS 718 777) (**fig 15**) has shown the high potential of such sites. This uncovered a sixteenth-century farmhouse that had been incorporated into the later buildings of the burgh as a dyeing establishment for weavers. Consequently, the remains uncovered by this project were able to reveal both the use of the land prior to the establishment of the burgh and its subsequent development as a centre for textile manufacture.[5]

Excavations in other burghs have also shown how the alignments of main streets have changed over the centuries, sometimes considerably. Earlier cobbled street surfaces and contemporary buildings may be preserved up to 3–4 m behind modern street frontages. The site of any proposed development or ground disturbance along the pre-nineteenth-century frontages must, therefore, be given a high archaeological priority. Arrangements should be made for the site to be assessed, monitored and, if necessary, excavated in advance of any development scheme. Similarly, any proposed ground disturbance of the streets themselves (for instance, for essential repairs, access to services, or environmental improvements) should also be monitored. This would apply to schemes such as the forthcoming full pedestrianisation of Main Street; trial trenches dug by North Lanarkshire Council indicate a large amount of disturbance from the previous pedestrianisation of the street in the 1980s.[6] Gap sites in the historic core of the town present opportunities for the investigation of the structural development of particular burgage plots and their place within the wider economic and social history of the town. A potential area of now open land that is earmarked for development for local

FIGURE 24
Former Kilsyth Academy
building, Shuttle Street in
1983 (By courtesy of RCAHMS;
© Crown copyright RCAHMS)

needs or amenity housing lies to the south of the present town centre, in Shuttle Street (**figs 9 & 15**). This area was within the historic burgh and archaeological investigation could provide an insight into the chronological relationship of this area to the present Main Street.

Archaeology is not only concerned with the evidence below ground; there is great potential in the existing standing buildings which, in their alterations over the centuries, reflect the changing life and fortunes of the burgh. Later alterations can disguise earlier structures, whose history can be revealed by careful recording and analysis before any major change or development. The recording of architectural features predating the twentieth century in the buildings adjacent to the Church Street parish church should be a priority. Archaeological remains associated with the former mansion house may survive under the grounds of the parish church.

While the present report concentrates on the area within the early burgh of Kilsyth, attention should be drawn to the other sites that fall within the bounds of the present town. Part of the site of Kilsyth Castle (**fig 3**) has been destroyed in recent years. The remains of the castle were investigated by Hugo Millar[7] and recorded more recently by the Kilsyth Academy Field Archaeology Group but it still has great archaeological potential.[8]

The area of the old parish church and the immediate surrounding site may hold evidence that could shed light on the little-known origins of the settlement of Monyabroch. The settlement extended to the east of Howe Road, the location of the old manse, but this area has been covered by housing and it is unlikely that much archaeological evidence of the former use of the site remains.

The late sixteenth-century map by Timothy Pont (**fig 4**) records Burnside in the area of the present Burngreen.[9] This settlement predates the foundation of the burgh but the precise location is unknown. Documentary research combined with archaeological excavation could reveal the origins of this settlement and its relationship with the burgh.

An archaeological evaluation undertaken in Fisher Avenue (NS 717 775), outside the southern boundary of the burgh, did not encounter any finds or features of archaeological significance.[10]

Further work on manuscript material relating to Kilsyth might point to other areas of archaeological or historical significance. Kilsyth's industrial heritage is particularly well documented, although the sheer volume of information renders it difficult to use. The key bodies who have either inherited or generated material relating to the town are the Coal Board, the various railway companies that operated in the area during the late nineteenth and twentieth centuries, Cumbernauld & Kilsyth District Council, and the Scottish Office Development Department.[11] More personal accounts of Kilsyth life might be found in the papers relating to Kilsyth's abundant number of friendly societies, in church records, or in actions brought by

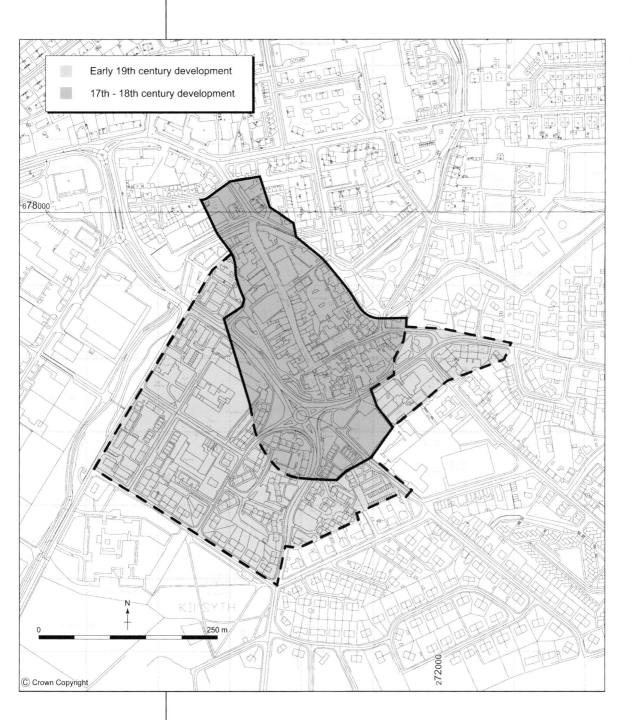

FIGURE 25
Colour-coded town plan
indicating areas of prime
archaeological interest
(*© Crown copyright. Based on
OS mapping. All rights
reserved. Historic Scotland
licence no. 100017509 [2006]*)

Kilsyth inhabitants before the Court of Session.[12] Other sources that have not
been fully explored include the local newspaper, the *Kilsyth Chronicle*, and the
photographic archive at Kilsyth Library. This resource was largely the work
of Mr John Gordon and the now-defunct Kilsyth Civic Trust; it is currently
undergoing revision by the staff of the North Lanarkshire Council Museums
and Heritage Service.

Notes

1. Cumbernauld & Kilsyth Department of Planning, *Kilsyth Local Plan Finalised Draft* (Cumbernauld, 1996), 34

2. Cumbernauld & Kilsyth Department of Planning, *Kilsyth*, 33

3. Cumbernauld & Kilsyth Department of Planning, *Kilsyth*, 19

4. *Buildings at Risk Register for Scotland*, SCT Ref No 2076. www. doorsopendays. org. uk/bar/index

5. H B Millar, 'Kilsyth burgh, farm-house, medieval artifacts', *DES* (1979), 34

6. Information and photographs of trial trenches kindly supplied by the Planning & Environment Department, North Lanarkshire Council.

7. H B Millar, 'Kilsyth Castle', *DES* (1976), 64

8. M Ponsford, 'Post-Medieval Britain and Ireland in 2002', *Post-Medieval Archaeol*, 37.2 (2003), 351

9. NLS, Adv Ms 70.2.9, T Pont, 'Map of the East Central Lowlands' (Pont 32)

10. E Jones, 'High and Low Craigends, Kilsyth, North Lanarkshire: Kilsyth Parish Evaluation', *DES* (2001), 71

11. NAS, CB series (Coal Board), BR/NBR, BR/PYB, BR/LMLN, BR/LNE and BR/BR (British Rail), COM11/22 (District Council), DD series (Scottish Office Development Department), including SEP4/509 (industrial development reports)

12. NAS, FS series (records of friendly societies), CH2/216 and CH3/976 (church records), CS series (Court of Session); see also a transcript of Kilsyth Heritors' Minutes, 1813–44, North Lanarkshire Council Archives, UK1/4/1. Digital copies are available at http://www. scan. org. uk/researchrtools/heritors. htm

Glossary of technical terms

ashlar	hewn stone with straight edges
broch	late Iron Age fortified circular drystone tower
Bronze Age	prehistoric period between the Neolithic and the Iron Age; *c* 2000 – 500 BC in Scotland
cairn	a mound of stones often marking a burial ground
carboniferous	yielding coal or carbon
cavetto	a concave moulding, making a quarter circle in cross section
corbel	a stone or brick bracket
cordiner	shoemaker
cornice	a continuous horizontal projecting moulding at the top of a wall or building
dormer	a gable with a window projecting out from a sloping roof
dripstone	a projecting moulding over a window or doorway
feu	a fixed annual payment for a piece of land
feuar	the holder of a piece of land for which a fixed annual payment is made
finial	an ornament topping a spire or gable
fluvioglacial	formed by the action of a river and a glacier
igneous	rock derived from magma or volcanic lava
Iron Age	the final prehistoric period, running in Britain from *c* 500 BC – AD 400, although the latter half is often termed the Roman Iron Age
lintel	a horizontal beam over a door or window
Mesolithic	meaning 'Middle Stone Age' and in Scotland representing the period of human settlement between *c* 7000 – 3500 BC
Neolithic	meaning 'New Stone Age' and in Scotland representing the period of human settlement between *c* 3500 – 2500 BC
nepus gable	a small gable carried up from the top of a front or back wall of a building, and having a small dormer-like roof of its own
stanchion	a vertical pole or beam
tambourer	embroiderer of fine muslin cloth
turnpike	a road with a barrier preventing passage until a toll had been paid, widespread in Britain during the eighteenth and nineteenth centuries
waulk	to shrink, beat or press cloth in order to make it heavier and more compact

Bibliography

Manuscript sources and maps

British Library, London (BL)

Map C9b5	W Roy, *Military Survey of Scotland*, 1747–55
	Glasgow University Library, Glasgow
Eph L/169	Edinburgh Committee for the Relief of the Unemployed
	Manufacturers in Scotland, Questionnaire, 1826
	(SCRAN 000–000–576–387-C)

National Archives of Scotland, Edinburgh (NAS)

CC9/7/1671	Testament of John Napier
CS129–63	Acts of Sequestration, Kilsyth Estate, 10 July 1716
E640/1	Rental of the Estate, 1716–19
FCN/1/1	Records of the British Railway Board, Forth & Clyde Canal,
	Minute Book, 1767–70
BR/KBR	Kilsyth & Bonnybridge Railway Company, 1883–1923
RHP 46699	Reduced plan of the estate of Kilsyth, 1856
RHP 46700	Plan of the estate of Kilsyth, property of Sir Archibald
	Edmonstone, 1856
RHP 82505	Plan showing ground to be acquired for extension to
	cemetery, 1908
RHP 85407	Plan of proposed railway from Kirkintilloch to Kilsyth, 1842
RHP 82526–32	Architectural block plans, subjects in Shuttle Street and
	Pirnie Street, Kilsyth
RHP 140023	Plan of Kilsyth, 1833

National Library of Scotland, Edinburgh (NLS)

Adv Ms 70.2.9	T Pont, 'Map of the East Central Lowlands' (Pont 32)
Adv Ms70.2.10	J and R Gordon, 'Sterlinshyr and Lennox. Sterlingshyre, wt
	a part of the Lennox, and sum of Clydsdal (Gordon 50)
EMS. s. 712(14)	J Ainslie, 'Map of the southern part of Scotland, 1821'
EMS. s. 623	J Grassom, 'To the noblemen and gentlemen of Stirling,
	1817'
EMS. b. 2.1(19)	H Moll, 'The Shires of Stirling and Clackmannan' (1745)
EMS. s. 712(14)	J Thomson, 'Stirlingshire' (Edinburgh, 1820)
Map. Fac. b. C18	W Edgar, 'A map of Stirlingshire, 1777'
	C A Ross, 'A map of Stirlingshire, 1780' [copy of original
	held in private hands]

National Monuments Record of Scotland (NMRS)

SGF/1930/3   Spence, Glover and Ferguson Collection: Kilsyth Academy, Secondary School

JS/6   Smeaton drawings

Royal Society, London

JS/6/64   A plan of the tract of country between the Forth and Clyde, proper for a (Smeaton drawings) *canal of communication by way of the rivers Carron, Kelvin etc. together with a projection thereof by John Smeaton engineer, 1764* [microfilm copy in NMRS]

Primary Printed Sources

Acts of the Parliaments of Scotland *T Thomson & C Innes (eds) (Edinburgh, 1814–75)*

Books of the Assumptions of the Thirds of Benefices. Scottish Ecclesiastical Rentals at the Reformation J Kirk (ed) (Oxford, 1995)

Cumbernauld & Kilsyth Council, Department of Planning, *Kilsyth Local Plan Finalised Draft* (Cumbernauld, 1996)

Gordon, A, *Itinerarium Septentrionale, or a Journey Thro' Most of the Counties of Scotland and those in the North of England* (London, 1726)

Handlist of the Acts of Alexander II J M Scoular (ed) (1959), no 347

Handlist of the Acts of Alexander III, The Guardians, John, 1249–1296 G G Simpson (ed) (1960)

Heron, R, *Scotland Described or a Topographical Description of all the Counties of Scotland with the Northern and Western Isles Belonging to it* (Edinburgh, 1797), 160

Kilsyth Chronicle

North Lanarkshire Council, 'Kilsyth Conservation Area Appraisal: 31/03/2003'

Ordnance Gazetteer of Scotland: A Survey of Scottish Topography F H Groome (ed) (Edinburgh, 1883)

Origines Parochiales Scotiae: The Antiquities Ecclesiastical and Territorial of the Parishes of Scotland (Bannatyne Club, 1851–55)

RCAHMS, *An Inventory of the Ancient and Historical Monuments of the City of Edinburgh* (Edinburgh, 1951)

RCAHMS, *Stirlingshire: An Inventory of the Ancient Monuments* (Edinburgh, 1963)

RCAHMS, *The Archaeological Sites and Monuments of Cumbernauld and Kilsyth District and Strathkelvin District, Strathclyde Region* (Edinburgh, 1978)

RCAHMS, *The Archaeological Sites and Monuments of Cumbernauld and Kilsyth District and Strathkelvin District, Strathclyde Region* (Edinburgh, 1982)

Robe, J, *Narratives of the Extraordinary Work of the Spirit of God at Cambuslang, Kilsyth, etc begun 1742* (1790)

Roy, W, *The Military Antiquities of the Romans in Britain* (London, 1793)

The New Statistical Account of Scotland (Edinburgh, 1845)

The Register of the Great Seal of Scotland J M Thomson *et al* (eds) (Edinburgh, 1882–1914)

The Statistical Account of Scotland 1791–99, Sir John Sinclair (ed) New edition D J
Withrington and I R Grant (eds) (Wakefield, 1978)

The Third Statistical Account of Scotland, 18: Ayrshire R C Rennie (ed) (Glasgow, 1966)

Books, articles and theses

Aitchison, N B, 'Townhead (Kilsyth parish), dun and hut circle', *DES* (1981)

Anderson, J and Black, G F, 'Reports on local museums in Scotland', *Proc Soc Antiq
Scot*, 22 (1887–88)

Anderson, K *et al*, 'Kilsyth Castle, North Lanarkshire (Kilsyth parish), building
recording, *DES* (2002)

Anderson, R, *A History of Kilsyth and A Memorial of Two Lives: 1793–1901* (Kilsyth,
Edinburgh and Glasgow, 1901)

Anton, P, *Kilsyth: A Parish History* (Glasgow, 1893)

Breeze, D J, *The Northern Frontiers of Roman Britain* (London, 1982)

Burns, I, *The Pastor of Kilsyth, or Memorials of the Life and Times of the Rev W H Burns*
(London, 1860)

Cameron, I B and Stephenson, D, *British Regional Geology: The Midland Valley of
Scotland* (London, 1985)

Campbell, A B, *The Lanarkshire Miners: A Social History of their Trade Unions, 1775–1875*
(Edinburgh, 1979)

Chalmers, W, *Old Kilsyth* (Ochiltree, 1997)

Clouston, R W M, 'The church and other bells of Stirlingshire', *Proc Soc Antiq Scot*,
84 (1949–50)

Coles, J M, 'Scottish Middle Bronze Age metalwork', *Proc Soc Antiq Scot*, 97
(1963–64)

Coles, J M, 'Scottish Late Bronze Age metalwork: typology, distribution and
chronology', *Proc Soc Antiq Scot*, 93 (1959–60)

Cowan, I B, *The Parishes of Medieval Scotland* (SRS, 1967)

Edmonstone, A, *Genealogical Account of the Family of Edmonstone of Duntreath*
(Edinburgh, 1875)

Gifford, J and Walker, F A, *Stirling and Central Scotland* (Edinburgh, 2002)

Gordon, J, *Kilsyth History Trail* (Kilsyth, 1980)

Handyside, R, 'Report on the Burgh and Barony of Kilsyth', *Reports of Commissioners
on Municipal Corporations, Scotland* (London, 1836)

Henshall, A S, *The Chambered Tombs of Scotland* (Edinburgh, 1963)

Hume, J R, *The Industrial Archaeology of Scotland, I: Lowlands and Borders* (London,
1976)

Hutchison, J, *Weavers, Mines and the Open Book. A History of Kilsyth* (Cumbernauld,
1986)

Jones, E, 'High and Low Craigends, Kilsyth, North Lanarkshire (Kilsyth parish),
evaluation', *DES* (2001)

Keppie, L, 'A Roman altar from Kilsyth, *Glasgow Archaeological Journal*, 5 (1978)

Lindsay, J, *The Canals of Scotland* (Newton Abbot, 1968)

MacGibbon, D and Ross, T, *The Castellated and Domestic Architecture of Scotland from
the Twelfth to the Eighteenth Centuries* (Edinburgh, 1887–92)

Millar, H B, 'Kilsyth Castle', *DES* (1976)

Millar, H B, 'Kilsyth, farm-house, medieval artefacts', *DES* (1979)

Millar, H B, *History of Cumbernauld and Kilsyth from Earliest Times: Including a Guide to Places of Interest in the District* (Cumbernauld, 1980)

Millar, H B, 'Kilsyth and the Couches' (Cumbernauld & Kilsyth District Museums Information Sheet, no 7, Cumbernauld, nd)

Mitchell, J F and S, *Monumental Inscriptions (pre-1855) in West Stirlingshire* (Edinburgh, 1970)

Murray, N, *The Scottish Hand Loom Weavers: A Social History* (Edinburgh, 1978)

Nicoll, J, *A Diary of Public Transactions and other Occurrences chiefly in Scotland, from January 1650 to June 1667* D Laing (ed) (Bannatyne Club, 1836)

Philips, W L *et al*, 'Croy, stone axehead', *DES* (1973)

Ponsford, M, 'Post-Medieval Britain and Ireland in 2002', *Post-Medieval Archaeology*, 37.2 (2003)

Pryde, G S, *The Burghs of Scotland: A Critical List* (London, 1965)

Rogerson, R W K C, *Jack Coia: His Life and Work* (Glasgow, 1986)

Simpson, W D, 'Notes on Lulach's Stone, Kildrummy, Aberdeenshire: A symbol stone recently found in Mortlach churchyard, Banffshire; and other antiquities', *Proc Soc Antiq Scot*, 60 (1925–26)

Smith, R, *The Making of Scotland* (Edinburgh, 2001)

The Scots Peerage ed. J Balfour-Paul (Edinburgh, 1904–14)

Thomas, J, *A Regional History of the Railways of Great Britain, 6: Scotland The Lowlands and the Borders* (Newton Abbot, 1971), 81

Cartographic sources

Blaeu, J, 'Sterlin-shyr', in *Atlas Novus* (1642)

British Geological Survey, 'Solid Geology: Airdrie', 1:50,000 (sheet 31W, 1993)

Soil Survey of Scotland, 'Systematic Soils Survey: Airdrie' (sheet 31, 1977)

'Stirlingshire', Ordnance Survey, 1st edn, 1:10,560 scale (sheet XXVIII, 1865)

'Stirlingshire', Ordnance Survey, 2nd edn, 1:2500 scale (sheet XXVIII, 1898)

Taylor, G and Skinner, A, *A General Map of the Roads, made out of Actual Surveys taken out by Geo Taylor and Andrew Skinner* (London, 1776)

Thomson, J, *Stirlingshire* (Edinburgh, 1820)

Index

Illustrations are denoted by page numbers in *italics*.